How Cannabis Saved My Sanity and Other Related Stories

© Ivor Morgan 2015

Printed and Bound by Lulu

HOW CANNABIS SAVED MY SANITY

It was 1966. I was a mature student at a local college. Things were not going well. Troubles and anxieties began to take more and more emotional time to deal with. Depression led to lack of concentration. Work suffered.

What were these increasingly debilitating problems? It seemed as if they had taken over my mind, leading to a lack of interest bordering on the apathetic. Well for instance, I was suffering from the effects of unrequited love – the girl in question rejected all advances. The term's student grant which I was eligible for hadn't arrived at the college office - there was a temporary bureaucratic hitch and money was running low. I had nowhere to practice my French horn – the sound could be heard all over the house in every room so keeping up the standard required to play in the local amateur orchestra was difficult. The house was being sold anyway, and the prospective owner didn't want to accommodate students. These and other long-forgotten problems seemed like an invisible heavy emotional rucksack burdening my back.

One morning a girl student in my group said to me 'I can see you're having problems - it's written all over your face. Go to this address after college and say Kate sent you'.

I had nothing to lose. At four o'clock I found myself at the address and the door was opened by a tall casually dressed man who invited me in as soon as I mentioned the name Kate. He didn't want to hear about my troubles but began to ask me a series of questions about my health, outlook on life, ambitions, progress towards thereof, relationships with other people, hang-ups if any.... and with a couple of cups of coffee the whole interview lasted for almost an hour.

I still didn't know why I had been sent to see this man. I was soon to find out. He asked me if I had heard of a drug called marijuana, also known as cannabis, and I said no. I had led a very sheltered adolescence - fundamentalist religious parents forbade us to attend or indulge in 'worldly pleasures' until it was too late to have experienced the normal transition from child to adulthood in the same way as the children of religious groups do today. I had heard the word 'spliff' at college but was ignorant of what it meant.

My host explained to me that this drug had a highly beneficial effect when smoked. If my problems were mental ones, he said, I would laugh but not at anything particular: if they were to do with bodily tensions I would be sick. He summed up this effect with an analogy – the expression 'sound mind in sound body' is well known; here a relaxed mind in relaxed body. I would experience a state of relaxation that I had probably never experienced before and that I would benefit by joining a small group this evening. I left with the assertion that I would be at his house at eight that evening.

The group was made up of five early-twenties people, four males and one female who, while not exactly hippies, nevertheless wore clothes that gave an eastern flavour to their dress, two wearing the then fashionable Afghan coats. My host and his wife made up the rest of the group.

After subdued greetings and getting into a comfortable semi-circle on the floor, with low music in the background, the serious business of lighting what was called a joint got underway, the cannabis having been burnt in an improvised tinfoil spoon and mixed into an extra-long cigarette made by an unusual arrangement of cigarette papers.

My most vivid memory of this meeting was that I gradually felt more and more relaxed until I was trying to sink into the floor and stretched myself out, oblivious to everything around me. And then I was silently talking to myself, telling myself things that I would have vehemently rejected if friends had tried to tell me. 'Are you really suffering from unrequited love, or is this an illusion? Does this one remind you of one you had jilted and felt guilty about doing so? Grow up.' 'Why are you worrying about digs? You said yourself that these digs were much better than the previous ones, so why couldn't the next lot be better still? Some will be moving to the same place. Come on, what's the problem?' As each of my problems were addressed and honest answers given by myself *to* myself – and I repeat - each answer and problem solved would have been rejected if anyone else had proposed them – they simply melted away and were replaced by an inner calm. Nothing could disturb my self assurance and freedom from what seemed very real problems which turned out to be in reality imaginary ones.

WHEN YOU SEE BEYOND YOURSELF

The meetings were never planned but seemed just to happen. I took part in several and at no time did I suffer any ill effects but never again experienced the total relaxation of the first experiment: it was as if the drug was saying that I had 'been there' and that the first deep relaxation which allowed me to be honest with myself and achieve peace of mind was enough – job done, so to speak. I still had a little way to go in knowing myself. Geoff's partner was very attractive and he was greatly envied – and she evoked great lust. One night, Geoff said something to her in French which was not quite right and I corrected him. This time I talked to my self aggressively. 'Why did you do that, you idiot? Do you think you impressed Fran one little bit? Why did you show off? You're pathetic.' I turned to him and simply said 'Sorry, Geoff'. 'That's all right.' And that is when

I realized the truth of George Harrison's words when he said that when you see beyond yourself, peace of mind is waiting there.

In the meantime, my new-found freedom from mental stress altered everything. I found a new girlfriend, the new digs were better situated, tootled on the horn occasionally and soon found no time to visit one of Geoff's 'Lebanese' evenings.

THE DOWNSIDE

Geoff was a salesman who began to take more and more time off from visiting clients. Other friends and I were becoming aware of this. One afternoon I had called in and by coincidence his boss called to see him: five minutes later Geoff was out of work. What was a pleasant relaxant for his friends and enhanced the pleasure of social gathering and perhaps listening to music had been abused by Geoff, in the same way as people detrimentally smoked too many cigarettes or consumed debilitating quantities of alcohol. Fran had a very good job with the NHS while Geoff wanted to mess around with boats with the intention of living on a barge.

A WORD OF CAUTION

The cannabis which proved such a boon to me was not the kind which is used by today's users which appears to be quite different and addictive. It also proved to be a life-changing experience for an acquaintance whose fascinating experience appears later in this little book.

As a medicine, pure cannabis proved to be a life-saver for me – not that I had suicidal tendencies in any way – but stopped the effects of worries and gave my life capacity for enjoyment a thousand fold.

WHENCE ADDICTION?

For occasional marijuana smokers the greatest risk of addiction comes from the (normally) cigarette tobacco that is used to host the drug to enable it to be inhaled. For this reason, the use of herbal tobacco, available from health food shops or the use of special pipes available from on-line stores that specialise in the relevant smoking accessories is recommended. The following experiences show just how much more addictive tobacco is than marijuana.

The girlfriend I'd met, had also used cannabis for relaxation and like me, had not been 'hooked' in any way. One night we answered the door to someone I'd met at Geoff's who informed us that 'Charles was visiting someone up the road and if we wanted some Lebanese, he would be there for the evening'. We simply replied 'Tell him thanks but we won't bother – it's drizzling'. Yet only the week before, we had been short of money and were dying for a cigarette and ended up filling a carrier bag with empty beer bottles from roadside bins and even door steps to make up the price of a packet of cigs – in early 1970, anyone buying a consumable liquid of any kind, had to pay three pence on each bottle in pre-decimal currency as a deposit which was then repaid on their return. On another occasion, having shared the tobacco with visitors, we walked over a mile to a main-road petrol station at two in the morning to replenish our stock.

In May 1968, the BBC broadcast a series of four programmes called 'Drugs in the Mind of Society' the first of which was given by Professor Stephen Rose. The fourth was given by a doctor who ended his talk by saying 'I am legally allowed to prescribe phenobarbitones to menopausal women, which is addictive but unable to prescribe the more effective cannabis, which is not'.

DANGER AND A SCARE

On one further isolated occasion we both decided 'to smoke a joint' and acquired the cannabis from someone who we thought we could trust. What occurred as a result, terrified us. As we inhaled the drug, it seemed as if something was burrowing deeper and deeper into our brains, exposing layer after layer as this chemical drill bore deeper, scaring us and making us fear for our sanity, until eventually it stopped. All we could do was wait for the effects to wear off and we both noted how pale the other looked. Never again, we both swore. Over the next two years, the author did use marijuana on two further occasions for a special reason which will be seen in the next section but one.

PETE'S LIFE CHANGE AND AN HILARIOUS STORY

Two years later, I was running an all-day cafe on behalf of a friend who had to go into hospital. One of the regular customers for cold drinks and the one-armed bandit was Pete – someone who was a tough amateur boxer but always looked extremely tense. He could demonstrate his power on a punchbag and in the boxing ring, but was shy when it came to authority. He said he had not had a raise for two years, but everyone in his department had and he didn't know how to approach the management.

I recognized from the tautness of his face how great his tension seemed and told him my story about visiting Geoff and would he like to try the experiment. He was keen to do so and I contacted a couple who were friends of Geoff's and who promised to come over every night to help Pete with his problem. It was explained again that if the tension was physical he would be sick: if mental he would laugh.

The first evening Pete was violently sick after about thirty minutes and a second bout of sick followed soon afterwards. He stayed for the whole two allotted hours and said he felt a lot better and could we continue. We agreed and the next night, Pete was sick a second time, just once but not so much. And again he felt a lot better than the first time. The third night was similar and on the fourth Pete had a very small amount of vomit at the beginning of the session and that was that. He felt great, he said, and his confidence was growing by the day. Most of the time we all sat in silent contemplation, irrelevant talking deemed just that. What was sporadically mentioned was the different images we saw on an abstract painting hanging on a wall and this subject is dealt with in a separate section.

The last night was and is memorable to this day. And with out a word of a lie, this story took four hours to tell. We were in uncontrollable hysterics after every word as the tale unfolded and we could see where it was leading but couldn't do anything to stop the laughter. Pete had a girlfriend and whenever she went to the lavatory for a wee, he would knock on the door and teasingly say 'I can hear you' which drove her wild. One day, she took him to her house for the first time and while he sat on the sofa, she disappeared upstairs. Pete thought she had gone to the loo, climbed the stairs and saw the helpful sticker on a door which read 'bathroom'. He crept up to it and said 'I can hear you' and as he did so, his girlfriend came out of her bedroom. 'Who's in there?' he asked in astonishment. 'My mother' she replied. It later transpired that she had half lifted herself in shock, wet the seat and her knickers and then her skirt as she involuntary sat down again.

Naturally, he fled and so did the relationship with the girlfriend.

The next day was Friday. To the surprise of his boss, Pete stormed into the managing director's office and simply said 'I am your best worker and you know it. If I haven't had the raise, backdated like what the others have had, I'm leaving and going to work at Baker's' The manager protested that the wages had been made up and he couldn't alter the wage-packets' contents. 'Well, unmake them' said Pete. He got them, came in, thanked me profusely, gave me ten pounds and was never seen again. We heard he'd won his last six fights.

When did all this happen? 1966 to early 1967.

And the reason for telling this story?

The hope that perhaps someone in the medical profession, especially that part which deals with mental health, may read this and realise that there may be a medicinal use for a much-maligned drug that would not only help a person's mental outlook, but also save a vast amount of health service money.

CANNABIS CONCENTRATION AND THE ARTS

An artist, musician, composer, playwright puts a lot of work into their creations and often has several layers of ideas woven into the finished product – understanding and following what are known as subplots in a drama enhances the interest and enjoyment.

Appreciating the fullness of the arts, is difficult in today's society because the amount of information our brains hold is a hundred times more than, say medieval man or even Victorian Britain man would feed into it - something as simple to us today as credit or debit cards and their associated security numbers and the stresses endured by most motorists on congested roads and the increasing amount of 'things to do and remember' make even the solitude of the bathroom a growing thing of the past.

As a result, when listening to music, looking at a great painting in an art gallery or watching a live performance of a play, most people have trivial thoughts or indeed worries which impinge on their concentration of whatever they are trying to experience – did I lock the car, did I remember to buy dog food, have I gone overdrawn at the bank – can suddenly dart into one's consciousness while, say, trying to concentrate on a painting by Rembrandt or Picasso, or listening to Beethoven or the Beatles or watching a live play in the theatre or the curse of modern entertainment – a television programme in domestic surroundings.

Examples – two - can be given from my own interests and I hope this will be relevant to the reader. Listening to a piece of music by the contemporary classical music composer Pierre Boulez, I found that I could not follow the four lines of musical argument in one section of the piece – the more I tried the more extraneous thoughts crowded in, filling the concentration gap with inconsequential garbage. A special effort was made to obtain a joint and I was surprised to realise that the relaxation experience was returning. One hour later, only the music was being concentrated on and the full impact of the composer's intention was literally revealed but even more important was that somehow I had subconsciously learned to concentrate better which made listening to music in this genre more rewarding.

The second harks back to a modern art painting by the avant-garde Dutch artist Karel Appel – blaze of colour and strange shapes which for some reason, I had to have and bought a print of it.

Looking at the painting, shapes began to form in the minds of visitors who saw this – a praying mantis, a submarine, a dinosaur head and neck, an aeroplane and many others – all impressions that some people saw differently to others. It was on Pete's last night that I placed this painting in front of the group and gradually we saw more and more objects, shouting out 'look, there's a slug.... and a bird..... and (wow!) a whale – where? – at the bottom in the middle'. Two hours of mostly silence were devoted to this and it was a memorable experience. Today, I cannot consciously find all these objects which seemed so clear as the relaxing power of the drug did its work.

Whether or not these experiences and the telling thereof have any use in any of the treatments of people with concentration difficulties or autism is for professionals to decide.

NOMADS FAITH CANNABIS AND PRISON - GEOFF'S STORY

As mentioned earlier, the author had met Geoff before but did not recognize the address – that occurred in a flash when Geoff opened the door and the results of that second meeting have already been recounted.

Two years earlier, I was a coupon collector for a football pools company and it was the norm for people to either renew their intention to continue the weekly gamble, or not. They would come to their door and I never got past their doorstep which of course, was perfectly natural.

Arriving at the last house, the door was opened by the person I now refer to as Geoff. 'Come in' he said and I followed him to his living room 'Coffee?' 'Yes, please'. Sitting there with my pools coupons, I couldn't help wondering why I was being so courteously treated.

He sat in the matching armchair and asked 'What did you want?' 'Before I answer that' I replied 'tell me why I am sitting here with a cup of coffee. You don't know me or me you and every one else says what do you want and either slams the door or takes one of these. But you have invited me in and given me a cup of coffee *before* you asked why I had come. Would you tell me why?' 'I'm a Muslim' he said 'But you're white!' 'Does it matter? Does God choose who can become a Muslim and who can't? And Allah has allowed me to buy this house for his people' 'But I'm not a Muslim...' 'It doesn't matter. You are one of his people, like it or not' 'How come *you* became a Muslim? Pretty unusual here.'

'I was in Morocco as part of my hitch-hiking round the world and I had no means of crossing the Sahara desert which was the only way I could get to my destination - Nigeria - at the time. Fortunately, a group of nomads had arrived in the village to water their camels. I had arrived at this small town by chance and a local man who spoke French and was aware of my problem, spoke to their chief. I was invited to travel with them as their destination was near the border of Nigeria. I helped with putting up the tents for the night and taking them down in the morning. But what impressed me was the strength of their faith that they would find water every day. Sometimes it would be after a few hours traveling but sometimes we would travel until almost sun-down without finding any, but they had unbreakable faith that water would be found and it always was. I wanted to have that kind of faith, to live with a certainty that a need would be met. I became a Muslim as far as language difficulties allowed and I was given a token copy of the Koran in Arabic as a gesture of goodwill.

The group grew as a couple of other nomadic groups joined – safety in numbers – and I discovered that one member spoke fluent French and I also discovered that he smoked cannabis, or hashish as he called it. It was against strict Islamic teaching but he was tolerated owing to his physique and language skills. I had tried it a little before, but here was a man I was going to spend at least the next few weeks with. It was a blessing in disguise because the daily life of my hosts was far removed from anything I had experienced before and the sheer relaxation helped me cope with the journey I was making.

I arrived in Nigeria with all my papers correct and still had money in the bank and took a bus to Lagos where I met a group of students taking a break. Buying and selling cannabis was quite legal under the then president whose name I can't pronounce and we did it openly. Overnight, this guy was deposed and General Ironsi took over. Immediately, cannabis was illegal and before we had time to escape, we were put in prison and deported back to England after seven days.

'You have your answer. So why did you come and knock my door?' 'I'm canvassing for Littlewoods Football Pools. You could win £75,000'. 'Well, as a Muslim, I'm not allowed to gamble. So thank you for calling.' I stood up and he accompanied me to the door. We both exchanged farewells.

UPDATE 2014

There have been several articles in the press this year about the evils of smoking cannabis. One front page of a British tabloid screamed. 'Proof that Cannabis is Addictive' as if the authors had suddenly discovered this startling fact.

Here are some examples. Note that reports such as the ones below always use terms such as 'habitual' and 'long term'. It will also be noted that none of the articles claim that the use of cannabis leads to the use of 'harder' drugs (its relaxing qualities result in the opposite) or have any delusional or psychedelic experiences either creative or destructive. This little book is published to promote discussion on the beneficial effects of the proper supervised medical use of the drug.

Cannabis can be Addictive, Report Finds

Although Professor Wayne Hall, a British expert on addiction, found that one in six teenagers who regularly smoke cannabis become dependent on it, he recognised that it was at the lower scale of risk for drug addiction. His other claims are that using cannabis during pregnancy reduces birth weight, and that teenage users do worse at school and are likely to be diagnosed with schizophrenia or psychotic symptoms. No evidence of this was given or his findings verified by other professionals.

The report was published in the national press in October 2014.

Cannabis Users have Lungs of 80 Year Olds

Dr Damian McKeon – a consultant in respiratory medicine at Ysbyty Gwynedd hospital in Bangor, claimed that users of the drug for ten years or more were turning up in the hospital's Accident and

Emergency department with a severe new form of emphysema (which affects breathing) and one patient needed a lung transplant. The doctor admitted that this report is a result of studying 8 (eight) patients at the hospital.

Use of Cannabis Shrinks Brain Size

The brain scan study of cannabis users by scientists at the University of Dallas, Texas, and whose conclusions were reported in the Guardian newspaper in November 2014, is one of the first to investigate the long term neurological impact of cannabis.

It was found that regular cannabis use shrinks the brain but increases the complexity of its wiring and connections between neurons. Dr. Sina Aslam, who co-led the research said that 'what was unique about this work is that it combined MRI techniques. Eventually, however, the structural connectivity or 'wiring' of the brain starts degrading with prolonged marijuana use'.

The team studied 48 adult cannabis users aged from 20 to 36. On average, the cannabis users took the drug three times a day.

Cannabis Legal in USA State

Colorado became the first state in the USA to legalise the use of cannabis and allow it to be sold as a recreational and medicinal drug. Full details of how, one year on from 2nd January 2014, the state is reviewing the effect of this legalization, can be found on the relevant sites.

In Honour of the Reggae King

The family of Bob Marley have launched a global marijuana brand named after the reggae king, which is being hailed as the first recreational cannabis brand in an industry that is on the cusp of a major boom.

Marley Natural will cater for both medical and recreational use, selling 'loose-packed' marijuana', vaporizers, pot-infused creams and oils, and will hit the market at the end of next year.

The company is a partnership between the late singer's widow, Rita Marley, his children and grandchildren, and Seattle-based, marijuana-focused, private equity firm Privateer Holdings.

THE END

Made in the USA
Monee, IL
03 May 2026

49437969R00020